Mum

Seriously!!

Teen-mum banter at its finest!

Copyright © 2025
by Tried and Trusted Indie Publishing

ISBN: 978-1-922695-98-7
All rights reserved.
Cover designed by msgdragon

No part of this publication may be reproduced, distributed, or transmitted in any form or by any means, including photocopying, recording, or other electronic or mechanical methods, without the prior written permission of the author, except non-commercial uses permitted by copyright law.

Also by M. S. Gregory

- Cousin Chaos: Laughing with your Cousins
- Sibling Shenanigans: Laughing with my Sister
- Sibling Shenanigans: Brother-Sister Jokes
- Mum Seriously?! Teen-mum banter at its finest!
- What Cats really Think: Hilarious Cat Thoughts, Jokes, and Conversations That Will Make You Laugh
- From Bark to Snark: Sassy thoughts from your Pup

For permission requests, address the request to the author c/o
Permissions,
TAT Indie Publishing
triedandtrustedindie@gmail.com

1. Teen: Mum, can you put my shoes on?
Mum: I don't think they'll fit me.

2. Teen: Mum, I'm hungry!
Mum: Hi Hungry, I'm Mum.

3. Teen: Mum, can I have some money?
Mum: Does it look like I'm made of money?

4. Teen: Mum, do you love me?
Mum: Of course I do!
Teen: Even when I eat the snacks you were saving?

5. Teen: Mum, why is my room so messy?
Mum: Because you live in it!

6. Teen: Mum, what's it like having an amazing child?
Mum: I don't know, ask Grandma.

7. Teen: Mum, I'll do it later.
Mum: Later is never.

8. Teen: Mum, you don't get me.
Mum: I raised you.

9. Teen: Mum, you're embarrassing me!
Mum: That's literally my job description.

10. Teen: You're ruining my life!
Mum: I made it, don't thank me yet.

11. Teen: You embarrass me all the time!
Mum: Good. That's why I practice.

12. Teen: You're ruining my social life!
Mum: I gave you life. Socializing is optional.

13. Teen: You make me eat vegetables!
Mum: Broccoli today, hero tomorrow.

14. Teen: Fine... I love you anyway.
Mum: Finally, some honesty.

15. Teen: Mum, can't you chill for once?
Mum: Sure... but then who would remind you to wear clean socks?

16. Teen: Mum, you're so extra!
Mum: And you're so easily distracted - perfect balance.

17.
Teen: Mum, you're so dramatic!
Mum: And you're so... loud.
Teen: At least I don't wake up the whole house snoring.

18.
Teen: You embarrass me all the time!
Mum: That's my superpower.
Teen: Yeah, but I don't see any medals.

19.
Teen: You're always checking my phone!
Mum: Someone has to monitor your chaos.
Teen: Or maybe just trust me like I trust myself... most days.

20.
Teen: You make me eat vegetables!
Mum: Broccoli is life.
Teen: Life would be better with pizza.

21
Teen: You always correct me!
Mum: Because you ask questions!
Teen: Or maybe because your answers are too long.

22
Teen: You never chill!
Mum: I'm chilling - silently panicking.
Teen: Silent panic still counts as stress.

23
Teen: You're impossible!
Mum: And you're... creatively challenging.
Teen: Wow, a compliment buried in an insult. Nice try.

24
Teen: You make rules for everything!
Mum: Rules keep you alive.
Teen: Then maybe make one that says I can skip homework once in a while.

25.
Teen: Mum, you're hopeless at texting!
Mum: At least I try.
Teen: Trying doesn't fix the fact that I got your typo in the group chat.

26.
Teen: You're overreacting!
Mum: And you're underthinking.
Teen: That's fair... but I'm still cooler.

27.
Teen: I'm leaving this house!
Mum: Fine, take the Wi-Fi password too.
Teen: Ha! Victory!

28.
Teen: You're dramatic again!
Mum: Says the person who just staged a fake exit.
Teen: Practice makes perfect.

29
Teen: Fine... I still love you.
Mum: Finally, some honesty.

30
Teen: Mum, you're so old!
Mum: And you're so... unoriginal.

31
Teen: Your rules are stupid!
Mum: Then show me how to survive on Wi-Fi alone.

32
Teen: You're always on my case!
Mum: And yet, somehow, I'm still your case study.

33.
Teen: You never listen!
Mum: I hear you... I just choose to wait until you realize I'm right.

34.
Teen: You're so dramatic!
Mum: And you're so late to everything. Balance restored.

35.
Teen: You don't trust me!
Mum: I trust you... to make mistakes I can learn from.

36.
Teen: I hate your jokes!
Mum: I didn't know sarcasm was a crime.

37
Teen: You never let me have fun!
Mum: Life is fun. I'm just saving you from reruns.

38
Teen: I wish I had a different mum!
Mum: And I wish I had one who didn't leave socks everywhere.

39
Teen: You're controlling!
Mum: And you're chaotic. Perfect pairing.

40
Teen: You're impossible!
Mum: Says the teen who thinks laundry does itself.

41. Teen: You never say nice things!
Mum: I just did - I let you survive another day.

42. Teen: Mum, you're the worst mum ever!
Mum: And you're the best argument I've ever had.

43. Teen: You're too strict!
Mum: And you're too clever. Perfect balance.

44. Teen: Mum, you're such a worrier!
Mum: And you're such a thrill-seeker - see how we match?

45) Teen: You're so old-fashioned!
Mum: And you're so... always updating.

46) Teen: You don't let me do anything!
Mum: I let you do everything - safely, mostly.

47) Teen: You're overreacting!
Mum: I'm reacting appropriately - that's different.

48) Teen: Mum, you never relax!
Mum: I relax - just not when you're testing gravity indoors.

49
Teen: You win... this time.
Mum: Don't worry - I'll lose tomorrow too.

50
Teen: Mum, you're always on my case!
Mum: And yet, somehow, I still let you live here.

51
Teen: You're so dramatic!
Mum: Says the one who yells at the Wi-Fi router.

52
Teen: Mum, why do you always embarrass me?
Mum: Because someone has to keep your reputation in check.

53) Teen: You're ruining my life with rules!
Mum: I'm just trying to make sure you survive it.

54) Teen: You're impossible!
Mum: And yet, here you are... alive.

55) Teen: You never let me have fun!
Mum: Fun is optional; survival is mandatory.

56) Teen: You're ridiculous!
Mum: Thank you, I practice daily.

57. Teen: I'm leaving this house!
Mum: Need a map... or a snack?

58. Teen: You always correct me!
Mum: And you always give me material for jokes.

59. Teen: Mum, you're always nagging!
Mum: And you're always testing my patience.

60. Teen: Why do you care so much?
Mum: Because someone has to keep you alive.

61. Teen: Mum, you're so extra!
Mum: And you're so... easily amused.

62. Teen: You don't get my music!
Mum: I get it - it's just loud noise to me.

63. Teen: Mum, stop embarrassing me!
Mum: I'm just saving the internet from itself.

64. Teen: You're ruining my life with rules!
Mum: I'm just making sure you have one.

65) Teen: Mum, why are you so dramatic?
Mum: Because drama is genetic - thanks for the inspiration.

66) Teen: You're always right!
Mum: Someone has to be - apparently not you.

67) Teen: You don't trust me at all!
Mum: I trust you... I just trust your decisions less.

68) Teen: Mum, you're hopeless!
Mum: And you're... still adorable.

69. Teen: You don't understand me!
Mum: I raised you. That counts.

70. Teen: You make me eat vegetables!
Mum: Yes. Even broccoli deserves love.

71. Teen: You never listen!
Mum: I hear you perfectly... I just choose not to panic yet.